Maestro

Maestro
Love Sonnets

Roger Armbrust

Parkhurst Brothers Publishers
MARION, MICHIGAN

www.parkhurstbrothers.com

Consumers may order Parkhurst Brothers books from their favorite online or bricks-and-mortar booksellers, expecting prompt delivery. Parkhurst Brothers books are distributed to the trade through the Chicago Distribution Center. Trade and library orders may be placed through Ingram Book Company, Baker & Taylor, Follett Library Resources and other book in-dustry wholesalers. To order from Chicago Distribution Center, phone 1-800-621-2736 or fax to 800-621-8476. Copies of this and other Parkhurst Brothers Publishers titles are available to organizations and corporations for purchase in quantity by contacting Special Sales Depart-ment at our home office location, listed on our web site. Manuscript submission guidelines for this publishing company are available at our web site.

Printed in the United States of America
First Edition, September, 2021
Printing history: 2021 2022 2023 8 7 6 5 4 3 2 1
Library Cataloging Data
1.   Author–Roger Armbrust, poet
2.   Subject–Poetry
2021-trade paperback and e-book

ISBN: Trade Paperback   978-1-62491-165-1
ISBN: e-book   978-1-62491-166-8

Parkhurst Brothers Publishers believes that the free and open exchange of ideas is essential for the maintenance of our freedoms. We support the First Amendment of the United States Constitution and encourage all citizens to study all sides of public policy questions, making up their own minds.

Cover and interior design by   Linda D Parkhurst, PhD
Acquired for Parkhurst Brothers Publishers by   Ted Parkhurst

092021

For the world's radio, television, and satellite channels
that grace us day and night with music of our classical maestros,
and the dedicated artists and orchestras who play it.

Contents

Chopin Throughout Night   8
Beyond Healing   9
Fantaisie Impromptu   10
Wallander   11
Sunfalls   12
Gentle Soul, Stay Gentle   13
If We Only Knew   14
There's Still Room   15
Old Soul   16
Queen Of The Netherlands   17
Prenocturne   18
Chopin And George Sand   19
If You Could See   20
Moon, My Soul   21
Beethoven's Bust   22
New Year's Eve   24
Valentine's Secret Formula   25
Sweet Surrender   26
Midnight   27
Schubert   28
Word Rhythms   29
Synthesis   30
Happy Birthday!!   31
Shall I Throw These Candles Away   32
Goethe's French Connection   34
Making Time For Mozart   35
March 10, 1785   36
Alone's Never Lonely   37
Maybe In The Next Life   38
Mindszenty   39

Power Lost   40
Mozart In Paris   41
Twenty-Fifth Symphony   42
Let's Dance In The Rain   43
Nobody Knows   44
"The Divine Bohemian"   45
Stepping Into The Day   46
Cell Symphony   47
Brandenburg Concertos   48
Speak Softly Of Miracles   49
Glenn Gould Recording Bach   50
Those Holy Old Forms   51
Haydn And I   52
Night Offers Itself   53
Maddalena Laura Sirmen   54
Hard-Won Times   55
Nannerl   56
Francesca Bertini   57
"Carmen"   58
Dark Morning   59
Moonlight Sonata   60
Venusberg   61
Red Priest   62
Solar Prominence   63
We Are Humming Grieg   64
"Hymn Of Praise"   65

Chopin Throughout Night

What's wrong with me? I keep hearing Chopin
in all my atmosphere. Within his notes
and silences I keep seeing you when
I close my eyes. Keep feeling you denote
the night—its essence of searching unknown
universes. Please understand. I'm not
listening to any instrument. One
with the dark and its mute subtle signet
of your spirit's presence, I now behold
constellations of your face, your smiling
mouth singing Chopin's nocturnes. If I told
you of your power, I've no doubt it'd sting
your senses, fuel your fears. So I'm silent,
lying alone. But the Muse is content.

December 23, 2015

Beyond Healing

Chopin's great etude's often called "Tristesse"
for "sadness" or "farewell". That doesn't make
sense. Depth of its meditation brings blessed
sight of you to me. Your healing smile takes
me with music beyond healing to peace,
even cosmic embrace. Were we to speak
right now (my sitting here alone to cease)
I might only repeat your name, struck meek
by his melody, your face overcoming
all. This may seem strange, unable to see
yourself as I do. Perhaps you'll play Chopin
and better understand—cantabile
like a human voice asking you perchance
to let my arms embrace you while we dance.

March 18, 2015

Fantaisie Impromptu

Chopin, his two great hands multiplying,
then returning, transposes ivory
keys into aural rapture. I'm lying
in bed, disbelieving. I start to cry,
suddenly a child, seeing Jack Carson
in glowing black and white, strolling across
the Prospect's screen, and me, a starstruck son
swept by his sad gaze, his lyrical voice:
"I'm always chasing rainbows, watching clouds
drifting by..." Now back, I'm praying, grateful
for this historic connection. Out loud
I chant, "Yes, Frederic, some motley fool
stole your creation. Oh, but let it rest.
After all, maestro, he stole from the best."

September 14, 2016

Wallander

He keeps challenging the fates, but the fates
have proved kind. To him, not the killed or those
he apprehends. Cat quiet, his eyes hate
the crimes. He studies their scenes, so composed
yet lonely. Then, tonight, we see him love
and be loved. She's a concert pianist,
gentle as a Chopin nocturne. He proved
gentle, too. Hopes to see her soon. They kissed
at the train. But now we sense he's running
out of time: age and inhumanity's
mad abuse. Memory's slipping. Cunning
and season can't help him. Fates' vanity
always decides: Love again, or escape
unwilling to his father's stark landscapes.

May 15, 2016

Sunfalls

I love how your long hair sunfalls over
your back as you sit before me, how each
highlight's rippling wave lets me discover
new depths of your beauty. I long to reach
and touch you, but know better. Choose instead
silent songs to you, music deep within.
Smile softly when you turn and smile, your head
nodding, your profile Rodin's temptation.
Eight hours later, I watch "Jimi Hendrix:
Electric Church". Feel us there: glowing stars
in Atlanta's thick July dark, transfixed
by his piercing howl-owl-owling guitar.
Now, late night Friday. Chopin's nocturne flares
the dark. I reach out, touch your sunfall hair.

January 15, 2015

Gentle Soul, Stay Gentle

Gentle soul, stay gentle through your currents,
your seeming endless storms. Breathe deep, convert
each fearful vision through prayer to advents
of peaceful imagery: angels' concerts,
loved ones gathered on smooth lake's sunset shore.
Know when Van Gogh painted his "Starry Night
Over the Rhone" he lighted it for your
eyes, your gentle soul. When Chopin takes flight,
glides through peaceful preludes, he's caressing
you. Listen to Whitman speak his poems
of joy, witnessing it, hearing it sing
in life's each moment—those calling anthems
seeking your response. When the Buddha strolled
his Eightfold Path, he knew your gentle soul.

October 14, 2015

If We Only Knew

If we only knew what we were missing.
If we just understood how brief the time.
If we would comprehend, not dismissing
our patient Muse's voice—unknowing crime
of running from Her—perhaps you and I
could sense in each cell great Chopin's nocturnes:
their early rhythmic freedoms guide our eyes
to caress each human motion, return
time and again to heartbeat, pulse, soft breath
of life leading emotion to create
new metaphors for your hair's braided wreath,
two tiny globes piercing your brow. Oh, listen
to his graceful leaps—passion on a mission.

July 11, 2015

There's Still Room

There's still room for beauty, room for rich blood's
rush to head and heart, for closed lips parted
in approaching kiss, for tongue's making good
a shy wish. That great night Chopin started
his nocturne, surely somewhere a stellar
galaxy reappeared, amazing eyes
of astronomers worldwide, reaching far
into cells of Sand's hand, guiding its rise
and fall over parchment, quill's tip
forming phrases in rhythm to music
flowing from the other room. Her soft lips
must have curved in pleasure, sensing mystic
connection, a night free of harsh quarrels,
passions bare as Andromeda spirals.

August 19, 2013

Old Soul

His great second piano concerto
alone would have been enough to save us.
Chopin, turned 20—caught in larghetto
of his demonic tuberculosis—
unmasking romantic masterpieces,
just now completes formal education.
Over halfway through life, no wonder his
old soul solar flares through his work, passion
and discipline caressing ivory
keys. Beautiful singers ignite phrases
to erotic height, his works a love story
of soft eyes and light. He'll move on, grace us
with life's pulse through music. We'll stray, bereft as
lost souls, until we hear what he left us.

June 29, 2013

Queen Of The Netherlands

When I come visit you, will you dub me
king, dance for me on Central Park's great lawn,
your favorite Beethoven symphony
or Chopin étude caressing our dawn
light and us? I'll humbly study your grace,
our world's only ballerina, revel
in classic glow of your van Honthorst face
in *The Matchmaker*. Who knows what level
heaven finds in existence. Can't it live
here with us? Back home in your living room,
secure in our privacy, will you give
me your lithe arms, wrap me in tender womb
of your caress as we did at the Leap?
Will you dance *with* me? Let our souls fall deep
until we whirl and meld to one, then sleep?

June 9, 2012

Prenocturne

This soft light glazing great boughs of green leaves.
This graceful light enfolding range of clouds
beyond glowing oaks. Horizon relieves
this falling light, descending slow as crowds
to sacred altars of night, signaling
to laughing, singing teens how now's their time
to wander home, bright voices regaling
muse of waking stars, of shy moon's curved rhymes
in mountains growing bold through rising dark.
Now do you understand, gazing out through
massive dusk, how Chopin wept, pounding stark
chords as though they were his last? How howls flew
from Beethoven's throat as he glared, regret
flowing from his frantic keys at sunset?

April 5, 2012

Chopin And George Sand

That Nohant summer away from Paris,
gentle breeze calming the maestro's scarred lungs,
filled them both with melody and rarest
colors. Hearing voices within, he plunged
into his *Polonaise*. She started her
book *Consuelo*, based on their friend Pauline.
Later she wrote how he wept,
complainer and endless editor while composing.
Delacroix painted their joint portrait, spoke
of seeking both color and form as one.
Frederic nodded. Next morning, he woke
to storms of coughing. Called out. Feared her gone.
She moved close to him, calmed his false alarm,
enclosing his graying form in her arms.

February 18, 2012

If You Could See

If you could see your beauty through my eyes
you'd greet each creature who approached with smile
so gentle none would fear you—your soft, wise
voice causing every beast to pause a while,
silently rejoice at your offered hand,
bow humbled head and feel your healing touch.
If you could see how your posture commands
the crowded room, sacred light, or how much
aura surrounds your motion, then you'd sense
Chopin's joy at composing sonatas
steeped in genius and filled with dissonance
igniting art. Or Schumann's cantata
sculpted from Thomas Moore, his angel's vice
exacting a tear to gain paradise.

January 30, 2012

Moon, My Soul

Full moon through my writing room windowpanes.
Moon bright white, blemished with cobwebbed shadows.
Moon, glowing molecule of great insane
idea, ignite my dark mind. I bow
to your bright sphere, dull blades of my open
blinds failing to slice your bobbing globe. Moon
recalling bouncing ball, rhythmic Chopin
conducting our moviehouse chorus. Soon
you'll dissolve from sight in this cloudy night.
Moon, my soul finding hope in darkest space,
make space for all of me. Earth without light
grows cold, threatens my entire kneeling race.
Before you're gone, lead us in song, some tune
inviting love's meager glimmer, oh Moon.

March 30, 2010

Beethoven's Bust
For William Packard

You've moved Beethoven's bust
from your main room—
crowded with head of Zeus
statue of Venus holding apple
bust of Shakespeare
framed Patchen poem
model's color picture
and b&w of old professor
all above bookshelves
filled with leatherbound volumes
of modern and ancient classics
their browned pages
patched with bright red and yellow
smears of your highlight markers
flashing each ultimate phrase—

to your bathroom's toilet top
where seeing it on Sunday
I recalled stories of him
reclused in dungeon-dirt room
ignorant of stench
from week-filled waste pot
and lack of light from lone candle
alert only to spirit symphony and
ink pen scratching on parchment
great phrases no one else had ever heard

New Year's Eve

WQXR celebrates its
classical countdown, flowing from Wagner's
Gotterdammerung to Berlioz's
Fantastique to Mozart in g minor.
Two hours from now their marathon will end
with Beethoven, always Beethoven. We
flow with them, love, turning on our brave bed
natural as earth through ages, flesh free
of clothing except for each other, warmed
by our passion and rest, and music passed
down through ages. We whisper how it charmed
kings and queens, how these melodies will last
long after we're gone. But this night we trust,
with knowing smiles, they flow only for us.

December 31, 2009

Valentine's Secret Formula

Honest, unconditional love and service:
not your usual relationship and care.
Yet, when led by spirit, what the mind deserves;
when melding life's passion, all the heart can bear.
What comes when you gaze at the moon? Beethoven?
Taylor Swift's rocket? Flow of night's ocean tides?
What aroma when you image an oven?
Your favorite pie? Where does your vision glide?
What feelings do you love to share? Athena,
with her owl-like eyes, protected her cities;
in her wisdom, led heroes through arenas.
What do you protect? Tell me: How are you wise?
Feel free to ask me the same. What do you pray
for through silent nights, or on Valentine's Day?

February 6, 2015

Sweet Surrender

Beethoven invades,
his sonata conquering
my gloom with moonlight.

Midnight

It's always our end and our beginning,
balancing our continuum. I hear
it strike and Patsy Cline's haunting voice sings
of walking and searching. Then Ed Poe's clear
chant echoes *Nevermore*. Now Beethoven
moves through his fantasy sonata. I'd
swear I see in the far field a coven
of ballerinas. Their lithe bodies glide
to his adagio through stark moonlight.
Surely this divines coming of our Muse,
she who fires poets' desire and insight.
Will she bless me with honest words? Accuse
me of fear and sloth? I breathe deep and stir.
I kneel, praying she'll let me honor her.

April 6, 2013

Schubert

Throughout your vast, short life (vast in music
and little else), you seem to fail: too poor
to marry Therese, sterile artist
circles and pro jobs tossing their heads, your
musicals kicked out every stage door. Still,
Salieri's lessons stick. You compose
with fire and gentle wind, creative will
amassing scripts to billow a warehouse.
Just months before death, you perform that lone
concert of your own works. Syphilis and
mercury clawing away, you postpone
study of counterpoint, your brother's hand
holding yours as you ask to be buried
next to Beethoven. At last you succeed.

January 5, 2013

Word Rhythms

By 40, tinnitus loudly ringing
him into brief rages, Beethoven failed
to perform his own concerto, bringing
a student to interpret all. When hailed
for his Ninth Symphony, vast applause fled
faint hearing, but greeted his tear-filled sight.
Undefeated when deaf, he turned instead
to writing conversation books, insights
flooding 400 volumes, word rhythms
forming sonatas of imagery,
how he perceived art, maestro's psychic hymns
for history's heart. Sloughing misery,
he composed till near the end, Late Quartets
including his Fourteenth: "my most perfect."

February 27, 2012

Synthesis

Interweaving our moist bodies as one,
we shape something new: perhaps lace of flesh,
perhaps chemical elements' union
redefining organic—cells enmeshed,
revolutionary biology
poets of later eras will record,
sensing how our tongues shun psychology,
spirits rely most on unspoken words
as our substance conceives to Beethoven's
nocturne. What do our half-opened mouths voice
so far from language? If ever heaven
were a higher stage of truth, make our choice
composed of calm and passion. Make it here
where our inflected forms meld, free from fear.

January 26, 2012

Happy Birthday!!
For Cecelia

Tell Beethoven to mirror Vivaldi!
Oh, play a happy piano duet!
Fill this Wednesday with music so lively
even professors will never forget
great experiences of the past year
leading to lively, memorable tales:
lounging on lush Florida beaches, near
panic on steep, torrid Grand Canyon trails.
A bountiful year for a beauty with
verve, blessed with amazing, classical gifts:
loving daughters and husband, a Greek myth
in the works, where all life flows like a swift,
perfumed wind, a symphony to seal a
soul's grand fate. Happy birthday, Cecelia!

January 13, 2010

Shall I Throw These Candles Away

Shall I throw these candles away?
These condoms and baby oil too?
The classical CDs we'd play
softly to frame our gentle mood
of love? We adored Beethoven.
Shall I throw these candles away?

Shall I toss the pillows and sheets,
this blue comforter turning gray?
The futon mattress where we'd sleep
those winter nights you'd choose to stay?
In candlelight your warm face gleamed.
I'd watch your closed eyes as you dreamed.

Dare I take down *The Odyssey*,
tear out the page where you wrote "Love ..."
or try to read Yeats' poetry
bookmarked with pearl-white envelope
filled with strands of your sunrise hair?
I'll hear your voice if I go there.

I'll see blue eyes in candlelight,
soft fingers flicking guitar strings,
feel arms enfolding arms at night,
recall words, laughter, countless things,
silences, how you loved to play ...
Shall I throw these candles away?

Goethe's French Connection

As Goethe turns nine, Voltaire pens Candide.
Some forty years later, the great German
has translated Francois' plays.
Then he meets Napoleon at Erfurt, tells of bans
with Christiane, hears of Bonaparte's care
for Maria over glasses of wine,
a Bordeaux the emperor longs to share
as the minister recites Voltaire's lines.
Four years after, he sits with Beethoven,
describing Bonaparte's ocean-deep eyes,
his penchant for belching, his beholding
to peppermints. Ludwig laughs in surprise.
Two years. St. Helena and no release.
Goethe reads of it. He smiles as if pleased.

July 7, 2002

Making Time For Mozart

Loined lines of his 17th string quartet
linger in clearing, stallions measuring
one another, then brief as twigs snap, set
and dash through rippling creek, legs treasuring
each stretch, hooves honoring each subtle step,
each leap, cut and graceful lean through forest's
impromptu avenues, narrow as sep-
ulchres. All this flowing throughout my best
self, and suddenly I hear Socrates,
Shakespeare, William Packard, and Bill Wilson
in chorus: *How shall we live?* As we please
or as some ghost-stallion carries us on
this sacred hunt? I hear Mozart's refrain.
I cry out deep within. Let go the reins.

May 1, 2010

March 10, 1785

Mozart, at Vienna's Burgtheater,
touches delicate keys, his andante
describing Constanze: gracious lover
and new wife, her deep eyes, delicate scent,
ebon hair flowing over his moist face
as their bare flesh rests after vast passion.
In the audience, Leopold—son's grace
lost to him—critique's Constanze's fashion,
dwells on the concert's take. He'll later speak
of gulden rather than genius. Wolfie's
bride caresses each note, recalls each peak
breath in bed, every gentle word. She feels
her husband's fingers unfold each layer,
sensing his dream phrases as joyous prayer.

October 28, 2014

Alone's Never Lonely

Alone never shares lonely's sad table.
Alone will dine only with solitude,
toasting glasses to all their laughable
bouts with pain, failures, snarling slights from rude
lovers. See how they gaze through dark windows,
smile and honor the half-moon—its balance
of shadow and light retracing earth's slow
evolution and devolution. Glance
at their swift feet as they dance to Mozart,
then stand still in silent grace. What Shakespeare
knew of alone he saved for Hamlet's heart
and tormented lips, too tortured with fear
to share solitude's faith. Caught, he'd cower
to blood's clot and the ghost's raging power.

December 15, 2013

Maybe In The Next Life

Maybe in the next life we two will grow
up together, grow old together. In
the next life, maybe you'll play piano
while I strum guitar, decide to begin
writing songs and sonnets ad libitum.
Maybe we'll live by the lake, with Mozart
and Hank Williams as neighbors, our sanctum
a refuge for Michelangelo's art,
Dylan Thomas's verse, his namesake's songs.
Draped around the fireplace, they'll gaze in space,
listen to your lyric voice all night long,
rise, record in their work your ageless grace.
Caught up in creation, they'll miss your glow
as you smile at sunrise. But I will know.

June 7, 2013

Mindszenty

Gazing out the open double window
at the steel-gray day, bare-boned oaks begging
in winter silence on the street below,
you stand in cardinal's garments, begin
breathing softly on your reading glasses,
brush them clear on your cotton cassock sleeve.
You've been writing your memoirs. *Time passes
slowly in exile*, you say. You won't leave
the U.S. embassy for fifteen years.
When you do, settling in Vienna, you'll
murmur the Vatican's betrayed you, clear
your throat, praise God, refuse to be a tool
of Rome. Told you're stripped of office, you start
your phonograph, pray, listen to Mozart.

February 15, 2013

Power Lost

Midnight, end of Christmas Day, and all light
vanishes sudden as gasp from townhouse.
Soprano singing Mozart flicks off. Night
floods living room. I feel my way like soused
reveler upstairs to find flashlight, stare
at blank computer screen. Then coiled serpent
of winter cold slithers through darkened lair,
my bare frame swept in sweat clothes. I repent
lost words for your sonnet, pray they'll return
with revived currents. Two days pass. Lying
under daughter's crocheted afghan, I yearn
to see your smile, gaze at candlelight, sing
oh so softly carol flowing from my
Walkman, pretend we're warmed by angels' eyes.

December 29, 2012

Mozart In Paris

At 22, fallen in debt, pawning
his watch, he refuses a Versailles post
as organist. He wanders streets, yawning
at offers from Salzburg, suffers the cost
of longing for Aloysia back in
Mannheim where her singer's rep is growing.
Hearing strings and brass flourish, he begins
his Paris Symphony, now bestowing
for the first time those lilting clarinets.
By June, Count von Sickingen opens his
home for a private performance. Plaudits
flow a week hence at Concert Spirituel's
premiere. July: He learns his mom's died. He plots
haunting movements for his darkest sonata.

December 19, 2012

Twenty-Fifth Symphony

Mozart, unhappy in Salzburg despite
Lucia Silla's nod in Milan, turns
to Sturm und Drang—his blending desperate
strings in searching awe, as if psyche yearns
to rush back to 9 Getreidegasse, both dash
and dance past his old neighborhood's columns
of shops with wrought-iron guild signs, flowered cache
of courtyards and passageways. How solemn
his sudden pause and reflection, then swell
of fearful wonder somehow transcending
to gentle cadence, as if calmed to tell
Constanze (who he's yet to meet) heart sings
when he sees her. How October wind spins
leaves around them, captured through violins.

December 12, 2012

Let's Dance In The Rain

Let's dance in the rain like tiny elves do
to their favorite small fairy combo!
We'll roll today's electric boogaloo
or fast-step our rapid '30s mambo.
Let's 4/4 time with Cab Calloway's jive
then swing dance to the Carolina shag.
We'll staccato, keep Flamenco alive.
Jealous nymphs will never call us a drag
when they see us jazz the hand dance and bop.
We'll join caterpillars and jitterbug
in the drizzle. We'll storm the Lindy Hop.
Let's ballet to Mozart's fugue. Cut a rug
through a shower to Elvis's rock 'n' roll.
Feel the downpour's power as we waltz, with soul!

March 8, 2012

Nobody Knows

how soft, curving line of your bare shoulders
makes me envision world peace: the crossbow
turned to a stringed instrument; recorder
derived from a tribal blowgun. Harsh bow
of a submarine hammered into arced
orchestra pit for offering Wagner
or Mozart. Who could understand how stark
light on your long neck could make me wonder
of garrotes morphed to diamond necklaces?
What wizard could wizen a hangman's noose
into lace collar gracing a nun? Trace
your gentle smile and see harsh Atreus
raising his sons as wise men, shunning kings,
forsaking war's despair for stunning things
like prayer, lyrics, Apollo's laurel rings.

February 6, 2012

"The Divine Bohemian"

Mysliveček—scratching at syphilis
on his nose—passes Fountain of Neptune,
tense psyche resounding with chords of his
new symphony. He squints, Bologna's sun
mocking his lack of sleep. He's on his way
to lunch with the Mozarts, give young Wolfgang
another classic model to portray
within his own work. Laugh how applause rang
with "Il Boerno!" at last night's opera.
Later, sun hidden behind Apennines,
Josef leans close to the candelabra,
its glow gracing his composition—lines
making history with a new quintet—
a work most historians will forget.

March 12, 2016

Stepping Into The Day

Stepping into the day, I study where
life's power waits. Where connection reaches
out. Never underestimate soft flare
of fingertips. Experience teaches
me this. Reminds me how sun's glistening
on grass blades welcomed Caedmon's eyes, inspired
Haydn to see *The Seasons*. Listening
to great Segovia's fingertips, fired
by Bach, glide over guitar chords through dawn
light, I recall how every small motion
is prayer. In midst of song, to reach and fawn
the dark cat's fur confirms how emotion
opens us to energy linking earth
and stars, to each cell's everlasting worth.

June 4, 2013

Cell Symphony

In *Harlequinade's* ballet, the clown's dance
steps seem stumbles. They aren't. While he moans blues,
Robert Johnson's slide guitar longs to glance
out of tune. Soul. Hillary Hahn would choose
Bach—her petite frame dancing in place—to
keep herself and violin honest. How
strange to think each of them—Hahn and maestro,
Johnson, clown—like you and I play right now
our cell symphony: consonance of one
hundred trillion units vibrating our
vital harmony. Yet we've just begun.
When we speak to each other of power,
do we sense ancient rituals? Do we
honor our continuum's chemistry?

May 24, 2013

Brandenburg Concertos

A century after Bach—struck blind, died
of a stroke—Siegfried Wilhelm Dehn stumbled
on the signed bound manuscript stuck inside
Christian Ludwig's files—a gift he grumbled
and never acknowledged. Nobly bowing,
Dehn saw it published, blessing to us all:
six Baroque vessels of cascading strings
softly caressed by harpsichord and calls
for basso continuo. Who here's fallen
in love (or hoped to) throughout the Fifth's
Allegro—violin, cello, flute blend-
ing, swirling, swelling? We celebrate thrift
of imagination, of dreams, feeling
magic depths each jeweled note's revealing.

December 18, 2012

Speak Softly Of Miracles

I want to speak softly of miracles,
love: of Haydn's *Miracle* symphony,
how its violins ascend—lyrical
praise; of Vivaldi's *Summer*—rhapsody
through harp's replacing violin's sweeping
storm; of Bach's sweet *Violin Partita*
transformed by eight-string guitar in keeping
with master Pound's imaged command: *Make it
new.* I want to whisper to you how strings
release to fingers' pressing tips—spirit
flowing forth in cords' response, creating
vibrations throughout our cosmos. Hear it
even in still air as we breathe right now.
Our mute lips touch—miracle of our vow.

December 3, 2010

Glenn Gould Recording Bach

Your thumbs and fingers appear to sprout three
inches when you first touch keys with gentle
strokes, then flash left hand in conductor's spree
near your face, directing your right's play till
left decides again to join joyous dance.
Were this my first glance, I'd deem you blind, eyes
rolled in trance, or rapt in some mad romance
with your Steinway as your head bows, rises,
bows again, face quivering, lips pleading
with keys and melody not to leave you,
never go, as if internal bleeding
will end all now, lover's last touch but true ...
then like spring rain you halt in mid-refrain—
critique with clearest phrase—begin again ...

March 19, 2008

Those Holy Old Forms

Morning sleet pelleting bedroom window,
creeping chill through my resting space, lifting
me from semisleep. I see London snow,
Haydn in his robe, watching flakes sifting
outside his hotel. *Whitehall Evening Press*
dubs him the musical Shakespeare. He fears
for his health and talent, primed by endless
feasting. Audiences amass to hear
him at the piano-forte. Outside my
townhouse, dawn light bejewels icy grass.
Glazed trees glisten. Wind creates symphony
of whispers, moans, rumors of what will pass.
I sit at my computer, day's rhythms
rising, inviting my internal hymns.

February 23, 2010

Haydn And I

are walking in Greenwich Village, and I'm
wearing my Sony Walkman; he's sporting
his powdered wig, recalling when he climbed
a wall to see the empress cavorting
in Vienna's court. "I was only twelve,"
he chuckles. But I can't hear him because
the volume from my earphones only shelves
any chance I have. Still, I sense him pause
in his stride. I look up and watch him frown
like a teacher seeing a pupil sleep.
I know my buddy feels I've let him down.
I hand him my earphones: "Here, yours to keep."
He slips them over his wig ... Eyes grow wild.
I know he hears *Die Schopfung*. And he smiles.

June 14, 2002

Night Offers Itself

Night offers itself to us, love, and we
welcome it—dark comforter covering
our bodies and psyches, process to free
us from day's splinters, from fears hovering
like Hitchcock's birds, bunched on wires awaiting
our moments of lost focus. But now I
focus on you, choosing music to fling
out our minds' gabbing committees, rely
on Vivaldi to lift us back, his lush
strings leading us to each other's tired eyes,
finding light within our near tears, a hush
embracing lips as if we realize
we need never speak again. Your fingers
touch mine. Deep velvet peace lingers.

January 10, 2010

Maddalena Laura Sirmen

Born four years past Vivaldi's death, you shared
his sense for composing and ospedale
life. Admired for the violin, you dared
to challenge those superior men. Sailed
to London after studying under
Tartini and wedding Lodovico,
romping with your cicisbeo, plundered
Europe's praise, playing your own concertos
for two decades. Later you wooed Paris
and St. Petersburg with your voice; some say
you failed. Still, you knew just how to caress
assets, storing wealth till Austria preyed
on Venice, driving the lira crazy.
You died poor, held by your lover Terzi.

February 7, 2008

Hard-Won Times

My heart hides behind flickering candles,
behind soft music like Jules Massenet's
"Meditation". I can't seem to handle
crowds anymore, those animal displays
of emotion from ordered violence
and surface chants. I work best one on one
these days—over coffee and confidence—
words meant for only you and me. Hard-won
times alone in the quiet dark, lying
curled like secure pups or baby sparrows.
When our heartbeats match, when constant crying's
never questioned, despair's poison arrow
lies broken on the floor. When we whisper
those brief, honest phrases: lovers' vespers.

December 13, 2014

Nannerl

She sits on the hill above Wolfgangsee,
hearing her harpsichord compositions
Leopold censored from recitals, pleas
from her brother to challenge him, reasons
too radical for her heart. Recalls how
she loved applause, those bright admiring eyes
of elite audiences when she'd bow
with her brother as one. Those precious cries
for encores. That was long ago. Her men
are all passed on: father, brother, husband.
Soon she'll return to Salzburg, six children
in tow, work as music teacher, demand
nothing from anyone. She feels fingers
ache for the dear keys. The lost years linger.

December 12, 2014

Francesca Bertini

Before the Nazis burned most of her films,
Europe swooned to dignified suffering,
her dark eyes mastering agony, whims
of coquettes, passion for lost wedding rings.
She preferred thorn pricks to rose petals, lack
of gesture to dramatic swoons. Shunning
makeup for soap and hard water, she packed
a hundred films into twelve years, cunning
leading her to out-earn Pickford. Seeing
her in *Tosca*, Puccini—shocked to hear
his music in the movie—smiled, pleading
to meet her. She refused. Snarling, she'd tear
up Hollywood's contract, marry Cartier,
retire for years till Bertolucci called her.

May 4, 2013

"Carmen"

On this day in 1875,
our fiery gypsy first appears on stage
in Paris to poor reviews. His heart gives
way too quickly, and Bizet dies at age
36 in June. Sensing failure, how
could he have heard our applause centuries
later, feel us suffering with José
as she hurls his ring in the mud; our wheeze
in low agony as he thrusts his knife
in her gut, weeps to her corpse, *ma Carmen
adorée!* that luscious music a life
in itself. How could he have envisioned
Tchaikovsky in November writing these
words of praise to von Meck: ... *a masterpiece* ...

March 3, 2013

Dark Morning

I rise in dark morning, lava burning
through my body, my mind's maniacal
editing session steeped in lost yearning
for you and yet beyond you, radical
voices screaming and whispering rumors
of what we've been and may become. I must
write it out now while fire brings light. No more
images spewing relentless. No rust
coating cold memory. Record the storm.
And yet as I write, I'm hearing again
Dvořák's *Cypresses*, feel healing calm
surround me, caress me through gentle rain
of violins, reminding again how
all brings prayer: rhythms of words, music's flow.

November 29, 2010

Moonlight Sonata

Daniel Barenboim preludes haunting
Almost a fantasy and I wonder
what your spirit senses. I hold daunting
image of your music—from blunt blunder
of a clumsy student or alluring
master's rehearsal or CD replay
or FM airing or, most enduring,
live concert-hall performance—how each day's
moment somewhere on our globe, your notes rise
in crystal showers, nourishing you there
throughout our teeming universe, your wise
glow always with us, our sighs and cheers fair
warning of your eternal energy
composing our passionate entity.

June 4, 2010

Venusberg

We are both hearing Wagner's *Tannhäuser*
overture live for the first time, its harp
and dozen waldhorns ascending to stir
our hearts. I turn to view your eyes, their sharp
aqua stare intense as Venus healing
all lovers, fair blond hair sweeping your bare
shoulders like a white phantom wave, stealing
me from this concert's cathedral to share
our bed blessed by gods, holy hands searching
each other's moist flesh, sealing yet again
sacred bodies' sacrament, flourishing
to join bold music's climax. Is it pain
in your eyes or joy? I study their blue
glow watching me. I know you feel it too.

February 5, 2010

Red Priest

Vivaldi—his years with Venice's
Ospedale della Pieta's orphans
refining lost girls into princesses
of music—leads tourists to cross oceans,
praising their ensembles. His disheveled
flaming hair tousling as he conducts,
tempts viewers to call him the "Red Priest." Led
to Vienna for commissions, he's dubbed
knight by Charles VI. His desire to compose
for Charles's court fades: the emperor dies.
The next year, so does the priest (I suppose
as clerics must) in poverty. Now I
listen to his "Concerto for Strings," sure
it shows us the Red Priest was never poor.

October 14, 2018

Solar Prominence

Burning plasma lifts from sun, its two forms
like lithe dancers caught up in passionate
music from eternity. Love, this storm
of space reveals all art, grace incarnate.
How is it you now play Tchaikovsky's great
piano concerto, its turbulent
keys giving way to sardonic cascades,
strings swirling through like excited children
to join the grand dance? How our telescope
captures these massive figures furling and
unfurling through magnetic fields. They grope
in cloudlike curls, powerless to ghosts' hands
controlling their entranced ballet, bodies
like ours in bed: cyclone, yet flawless peace.

October 4, 2008

We Are Humming Grieg

as we lounge among Mount Floyen's trees, love,
looking down on Bergen's inlet, the sun
drifting like a blazing krone from above
into the bay's glaze of dark wine. Someone's
cued the town's lighting director, her art
vying with arriving stars. You recall
our touring fjords at dawn, want to start
again at daybreak, challenge *de syv djell.*
I laugh, then fall into your North Sea eyes,
fathomless in their joy. Just what lyric
pieces would he compose, do you surmise,
were he gazing as I at Homeric
wonder of your face? Make me a Viking,
perhaps, or an adoring mountain king?

January 12, 2012

"Hymn Of Praise"

Mendelssohn possesses it, doesn't he:
Sense of presence leading to reverence,
not so much awaking as reverie
evolving to understanding, essence
of living within all. Listen how his
Adagio religioso, strings
flowing, envisions Gutenberg, spirit's
caress of sudden insight revealing
moveable type—its releasing knowledge
from tight fists of monks, pushing past Latin
to each nation's vernacular: his pledge
of spreading new words of men and women
throughout our earth. As you touch each book's page
recall his genius, gift to every age.

October 11, 2018

If you have enjoyed this book of poetry, visit
www.parkhurstbrothers.com
for more books by Roger Armbrust.